I0816529

Utah

BY MARTHA LONDON

CONTENT CONSULTANT
Jedediah Rogers, PhD
Utah and western American historian

An Imprint of Abdo Publishing
abdobooks.com

abdobooks.com

Published by Abdo Publishing, a division of ABDO, PO Box 398166, Minneapolis, Minnesota 55439.

Printed in the United States of America, North Mankato, Minnesota.
052022
092022

Cover Photo: Shutterstock Images
Interior Photos: Kevin Ruck/Shutterstock Images, 4–5; Larisa Duka/iStockphoto, 6, 45; Shutterstock Images, 9, 19 (flag), 30–31; Red Line Editorial, 11 (Utah), 11 (USA); Abbie Warnock-Matthews/Shutterstock Images, 12–13; A. J. Russell/Smith Archive/Alamy, 15, 43; L. Tom Perry Special Collections/Harold B. Lee Library/Brigham Young University, 17; Alfie Photography/Shutterstock Images, 19 (elk); Mel Kowasic/Shutterstock Images, 19 (gull); Michael Sy/Shutterstock Images, 19 (lily); Don Mammoser/Shutterstock Images, 19 (aspen); iStockphoto, 22–23, 24; Jay Pierstorff/Shutterstock Images, 27; Yegoro V/Shutterstock Images, 33; Arthur Mola/Invision/AP/Shutterstock Images, 35; Natacha Pisarenko/AP Images, 36–37; Josh Ewing/iStockphoto, 41

Editor: Angela Lim
Series Designer: Joshua Olson

Library of Congress Control Number: 2021951546

Publisher's Cataloging-in-Publication Data

Names: London, Martha, author.
Title: Utah / by Martha London
Description: Minneapolis, Minnesota : Abdo Publishing, 2023 | Series: Core library of US states | Includes online resources and index.
Identifiers: ISBN 9781532197864 (lib. bdg.) | ISBN 9781098270629 (ebook)
Subjects: LCSH: U.S. states--Juvenile literature. | Western States (U.S.)--Juvenile literature. | Utah--History--Juvenile literature. | Physical geography--United States--Juvenile literature.
Classification: DDC 979.2--dc23

Population demographics broken down by race and ethnicity come from the 2019 census estimate. Population totals come from the 2020 census.

CONTENTS

CHAPTER ONE

THE BEEHIVE STATE

Skiers strap on their boots. They carry their skis to the lift. The Sundance Mountain Resort in Utah has some of the best skiing and snowboarding around.

Powdery snow flies into the air. The skiers cut back and forth as they slide down the mountain. Pine, spruce, and aspen trees tower on each side of the run. Sun reflects off the white snow. At the bottom, the skiers are ready for another run down the mountain.

Park City, Utah, is located near the Wasatch Range.

Utah is famous for unique red rock formations.

ABOUT UTAH

Utah is in the western United States. It is known for having a hot, dry climate. Most of the state's water comes from its winter snowfall. Melting snow from the Wasatch Range feeds into streams and lakes such as the Great Salt Lake. Utah has deserts with rock formations that do not exist anywhere else.

Utah shares a border with six other states. Idaho and Wyoming lie to the north. Nevada makes Utah's western border. The southeastern corner is part of the Four Corners region. The Four Corners is the only place in the United States where the borders of four states touch. These states are Utah, Arizona, New Mexico, and Colorado.

Most of Utah's biggest cities lie to the west of the Wasatch Range. This region is known as the Wasatch Front. Ogden, Provo, and Salt Lake City are all located in this region. Approximately 80 percent of Utah's population lives in the Wasatch Front. Southern Utah has fewer cities.

PERSPECTIVES

A RACING TRADITION

The Bonneville Salt Flats used to be an ancient desert lake. As the water dried up, salt and minerals in the water were left behind. This created the salt flats seen in Utah today. Racers have used the Bonneville Salt Flats as a racetrack for more than 100 years. They have reached 500 miles per hour (800 km/h) on the track. But the salt flats are in danger. The crust is getting thinner. Brenda Bowen is a scientist who studies the salt flats. She believes the salt flats could recover. "I would say leave it alone for a few years. Don't come out here. Don't drive on it when it's wet, give it a minute, and let's see where it gets to."

Many different people and cultures made Utah the state it is today. Historically European and American Indian traditions were the dominant cultural influences. The earliest peoples came to the region about 11,000 years ago. Members of the Church of Jesus Christ of Latter-day Saints arrived in the mid-1800s. Latter-day Saints are also called Mormons. Today these two major influences can be seen across Utah. But Utah is also home to other ethnic groups. These groups have important roles in Utah's history and continue to shape the state's identity today.

The US government recognizes eight American Indian tribes in Utah today. Utah gets its name from the Ute tribe. *Ute* means "people of the mountains."

Mormon influence led to the state's nickname, the Beehive State. When Latter-day Saints came to the region, they used the beehive as their symbol. Mormon heritage is visible at the Salt Lake Temple

The Salt Lake Temple is one of the most iconic buildings in Salt Lake City.

WHAT'S IN A NICKNAME?

Brigham Young is an important person in the Mormon religion. He is credited with giving Utah its Beehive State nickname. Bees are important symbols in the Mormon holy book, *The Book of Mormon*. When Young arrived in the Utah region, he chose the name "Deseret" for the area. It is the word for honeybee in *The Book of Mormon*. He hoped the name would inspire people to work together like bees. This also inspired the creation of Utah's state motto, Industry. Latter-day Saints had to rely on their "industry" or hard work in order to bring new life to the desert.

in Salt Lake City. The temple is a place of worship for Latter-day Saints. Salt Lake City is Utah's most populated city and the capital of the state. It sits near the Great Salt Lake.

From deserts to the Great Salt Lake, the state has many landscapes. It has big cities. There are open grasslands for sheep and cattle. Natural arches and canyons dot the desert landscapes.

MAP OF UTAH

Utah has many important cities and famous landmarks. What does this map show you about the locations of Utah's major cities? How does this map help you understand Utah's unique geography?

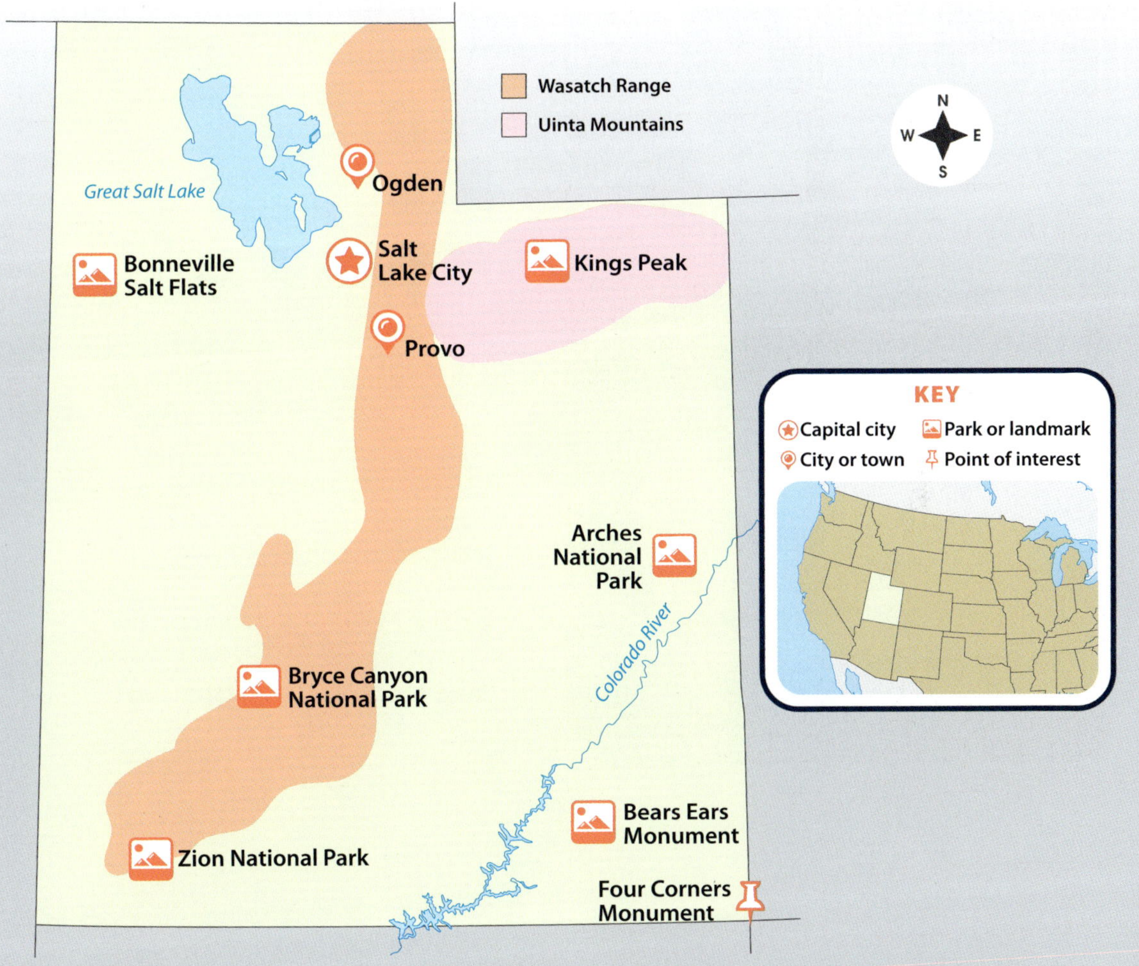

CHAPTER TWO

HISTORY OF UTAH

People have been living in Utah since approximately 9000 BCE. These people were hunters and gatherers. They made baskets for collecting plants. They also made stone-tipped spears for hunting. They created rock carvings inside caves that showed their histories.

The Fremont culture developed between 1,500 and 2,500 years ago. These peoples began to farm. But most people continued to hunt and gather for food. The Fremont peoples

Historians study rock carvings to learn about the lives of early people in the Utah region.

PERSPECTIVES

STUDYING PETROGLYPHS

Petroglyphs are paintings and carvings on rock walls. Utah has many petroglyphs. People made them thousands of years ago. Images show people hunting animals and doing other activities. The images help scientists understand how people lived in the past. They are also important to American Indian nations. Many nations have traveled to the same locations for generations. Their ancestors carved or painted the rock walls. Dorena Martineau is a member of the Paiute Indian Tribe of Utah. She explained the images this way: "Even though we can't read the petroglyphs, they're important stories from our past, small and big. It's like our library."

lived in permanent houses in northern Utah. They also made buildings to store food.

Ancestral Pueblo culture also developed around 500 BCE. But the Ancestral Pueblo lived in southern Utah. They relied on farming and grew corn, beans, and other crops. Around 1150 CE these people began building homes into the sides of cliffs. Historians have also found weavings and pottery from this time.

The Ute tribe lived in the central and eastern regions of Utah.

In 1200 CE Numic-speaking peoples entered the Utah region. Over time, these Numic groups became some of the American Indian nations that people recognize today. The Ute, Shoshone, and Paiute are just a few examples.

Pueblo peoples lived in the region for 600 years before the first white explorers arrived. European and American fur trappers built trading posts in the 1820s. In the late 1840s, settlers began building permanent settlements.

BECOMING A STATE

The first Latter-day Saints began arriving in the area in 1847. They settled near the Great Salt Lake, where there was water for agriculture. By 1860 more than 40,000 Latter-day Saints had come to the region.

Latter-day Saints came to Utah from across Europe and the United States. Some were from the US South. They brought enslaved Black people with them. Slavery was legal in this region from 1852 to 1862.

There were many conflicts between Latter-day Saints and other peoples. Some arguments were with American Indian nations. Latter-day Saints took over American Indian lands and disrupted their lifestyles.

There were also conflicts between Mormon leaders and the federal government. The US government did not agree with some Mormon practices, such

Brigham Young was the governor of the Utah Territory from 1850 to 1857.

as polygamy. This practice allowed men to have multiple wives. President James Buchanan wanted a nonreligious leader to replace Brigham Young, the Mormon governor of Utah. In 1857 Buchanan sent the US Army to remove Young. This was the start of the Utah War. It ended in 1858, after Young had given up his title as governor.

The movement of US troops into the area helped open mines. For example, General Patrick Edward

Connor encouraged his men to mine for valuable minerals. The mines brought people who were not Latter-day Saints to the territory.

As more white settlers arrived, conflicts with American Indians arose again. The US government forced American Indian leaders to sign treaties. The Ute signed a treaty in 1865. They agreed to move onto a reservation in northeastern Utah.

Utah's first attempt at statehood was in 1849. The US government rejected early attempts at statehood because of the practice of polygamy. Latter-day Saints had to officially ban the practice before Utah could become a state. In 1890 the Church of Jesus Christ of Latter-day Saints published a document that banned polygamy. After decades of trying to gain statehood, Utah officially became a state on January 4, 1896.

UTAH IN THE 1900s

Utah's mines brought many people into the state. However, mining could be dangerous. In 1900 a deadly

UTAH

QUICK FACTS

Each US state has its own unique history and culture. How do Utah's state nickname and motto represent its history? Did you find any of Utah's state symbols surprising?

Abbreviation: UT
Nickname: The Beehive State
Motto: Industry
Date of statehood: January 4, 1896
Capital: Salt Lake City
Population: 3,271,616
Area: 84,897 square miles (219,882 sq km)

STATE SYMBOLS

State animal
Rocky Mountain elk

State flower
Sego lily

State bird
California gull

State tree
Quaking aspen

explosion at a Utah coal mine killed at least 200 workers. This disaster forced state and federal governments to create safety measures to protect miners.

TOPAZ RELOCATION CENTER

During World War II, the US government was distrustful of the people of Japanese descent living in the United States. It unfairly forced many Japanese Americans to leave their homes. They were moved to concentration camps such as the Topaz Relocation Center in Utah. They had very little freedom in these camps. They experienced violence from guards. The buildings they were forced to live in offered little protection from harsh Utah weather. Topaz closed in October 1945, after the end of the war.

Utah played an important role in World War II (1939–1945). During this time, the United States was at war with Japan. The United States dropped two atomic bombs on Japan to end the war. The pilots who dropped the bombs had trained in Utah. They practiced dropping fake bombs over Utah's deserts.

STRAIGHT TO THE SOURCE

The Ancestral Pueblo lived in southern Utah for 1,000 years. Then they moved. They left behind amazing cliff dwellings. Craig Childs, an author who writes about archaeology, believes the cliffs hold answers as to why the Ancestral Pueblo left:

> *When rainfall was reliable . . . the [Ancestral Pueblo] built their roads and monuments. Then, when the population reached its highest level, a severe drought hit. Malnutrition coursed through villages. Warfare broke out. Settlements that once stood proudly atop mesas fell to ruins. . . .*
>
> *Perched on ledges and tucked into cracks of this canyon are the ruins of cliff dwellings. . . . But you don't live in these cliffs unless you have to. For all of its artful construction, the dwelling is a sign that they were moving to the last water sources.*

Source: Craig Childs. "Tracking a Vanished Civilization in the Southwest," *NPR*, July 12, 2007, npr.org. Accessed 2 April 2021.

WHAT'S THE BIG IDEA?

Take a close look at this passage. What is the main connection being made between the cliff dwellings and the Ancestral Pueblo? What can you tell about the importance of the cliff dwellings to these people?

CHAPTER THREE

GEOGRAPHY AND CLIMATE

Utah has many different landscapes. To the west of the Wasatch Range lies the Great Basin. The rivers in this region flow into lakes or dry up. The Great Basin includes the Great Salt Lake Desert and salt flats. Mountains mark the boundaries of the Great Basin. These peaks hold many minerals such as copper and gold. The Great Basin region is desertlike. It gets very little rain, and summers can be hot.

Utah's Great Salt Lake is located in the Great Basin region.

Rock formations called hoodoos can be seen at Bryce Canyon National Park.

The Colorado Plateau covers the eastern half of Utah. A plateau is a raised area of land with a flat top. The rivers in this region flow into the Colorado River, which is the longest river in the state. The Colorado River runs for approximately 1,450 miles (2,330 km) across seven states. Utah is famous for the red rock, canyons, and national parks on the Colorado Plateau.

Utah's northeast is dominated by a region of the Rocky Mountains known as the Middle Rockies.

This region contains the Uinta Mountains. Kings Peak, Utah's highest point in elevation, is in this mountain range.

Glaciers helped shape the Middle Rockies. Glaciers are massive pieces of ice and snow. As the glaciers melted, they dragged pieces of rock away from the mountains. This created valleys and other unique formations.

PERSPECTIVES

DIVERSE CLIMATES

Approximately 33 percent of Utah is desert. The West Desert makes up Utah's Great Basin region. The Canyonlands in the southeastern part of the state is another desert region. But Utah is more than just desert. Some mountain regions get more than 55 inches (140 cm) of rain and snow a year. Alana Brophy studies the weather in Utah. She says, "It's no doubt we have the 'Greatest Snow on Earth' in the state of Utah. If you have recreated in our powder, you know it's different from the wet, heavy snow we see in other parts of the country."

One of Utah's most famous features is the Great Salt Lake. This lake is what is left of a much larger ancient body of water.

Lake Bonneville formed 25,000 years ago. The lake was once more than 1,000 feet (305 m) deep. But there was a huge flood 15,000 years ago. The water from Lake Bonneville rushed into a nearby river. The water level in Lake Bonneville dropped by more than 300 feet (90 m). Changes in Utah's climate caused more lake water to evaporate. The salt in Lake Bonneville became more concentrated. This is what caused the Great Salt Lake to be so salty. It also created the Bonneville Salt Flats.

PLANTS AND ANIMALS

Plants and animals in the Great Basin region are used to the dry climate. The creosote bush is a desert plant. It has waxy leaves that prevent water from leaving the plant. During especially dry periods, creosote bushes drop their leaves to save energy. These plants also have a taproot, which is a main root that reaches deep underground. It helps the plant collect more water.

The prairie falcon is one of many desert animals. It relies on its speed to hunt over the open desert

A prairie falcon's coloring helps it blend into the cliffs where it nests.

landscape. It flies close to the ground and catches its prey by surprise.

Plants in the mountains are able to withstand many types of weather. At high elevations the temperature can change quickly. It may be very windy. Blue spruce trees are able to survive these extreme weather conditions. They need less water than other types of spruce trees. They can grow in colder temperatures. Blue spruce trees are common in the mountain regions of Utah for these reasons.

Climate change threatens all areas of Utah. Temperatures around the world are rising. The risk of drought and wildfires increases as a result. Climate change also increases the risk of extreme rain events. Land cannot absorb water quickly after a period of drought. Extreme rain events may lead to flash floods.

THE QUAKING GIANT

Quaking aspens have connected root systems. Pando is the largest system of connected quaking aspens in Utah. It is also one of the oldest living things on Earth. Pando covers 106 acres (43 ha). Scientists believe its roots are 80,000 years old. Pando is made up of more than 40,000 trees. Some of them are 130 years old. Scientists note that Pando is dying. New trees grow from the root system. But the old trees are dying at a faster rate. Deer and livestock may graze on young shoots before they can grow into full trees.

STRAIGHT TO THE SOURCE

Natalie Gochnour served with the Environmental Protection Agency in the early 2000s. She worked with a government committee in 2019. Together, they created a list of environmental recommendations for Utah lawmakers. In a statement about air quality, the committee wrote:

> *All Utahns deserve to breathe clean air, enjoy the splendors of Utah's natural wonders, achieve their potential and contribute to society. Breathing polluted air, even for short periods, seriously affects the health of every Utahn. . . . The stakes are high, and our actions to reduce air pollution are crucially important to ensure a healthy and productive population, a prosperous and growing economy, and a beautiful and functional outdoor environment that serves multiple needs.*

Source: Natalie Gochnour. "The Utah Roadmap: Positive Solutions on Climate and Air Quality," *University of Utah*, January 2020, gardner.utah.edu. Accessed 5 October 2020.

CONSIDER YOUR AUDIENCE

Adapt this passage for a different audience, such as your principal or friends. Write a blog post conveying this same information for the new audience. How does your post differ from the original text and why?

CHAPTER FOUR

RESOURCES AND ECONOMY

Transportation is a big industry for Utah. This is because it is located near many other western states. Salt Lake City is nicknamed the Crossroads of the West. Trucking companies can serve many regions from one central location. It is easy to reach several states from Salt Lake City. Companies do not need to have extra buildings.

Salt Lake City is also attractive to businesses for another reason. The city

The Wasatch Range can be seen from Salt Lake City.

has low taxes. This makes it easier for businesses to make money.

UTAH'S TECH INDUSTRY

Utah's technology industry is one of the fastest-growing of any US state. There is a tech company located in almost every county in Utah. But most tech jobs are located near Salt Lake City. Tech jobs include things such as designing software programs for computers or manufacturing hardware. Nearly one in seven Utahns has a job in the tech industry. The industry brings new residents to the state. But some experts worry that this will create other problems. Some predict that there is not enough housing in Utah's major cities to support this growth.

MINING AND TOURISM

Outside of the Wasatch Front, agriculture and mining continue to be big businesses. Utah has many natural resources, including coal and oil. The state also has many precious metals such as gold, silver, and copper. These materials are used in many industries. Medical and technology companies use these metals. In the past, companies mined

The Kennecott Copper Mine located near Salt Lake City is one of the largest open-pit copper mines in the world.

uranium in the Four Corners region. Uranium can be used as fuel in nuclear power plants. People also collect salt from the Great Salt Lake.

PERSPECTIVES

URANIUM WASTE

Utah does not have any active uranium mines as of 2020. But the state does have a uranium processing mill that takes uranium waste from other countries. It turns the waste into usable uranium. However, research shows that less than 1 percent of the waste material is usable. Tim Peterson works for the Grand Canyon Trust. In an interview he said, "We're concerned that the White Mesa mill [is treated as] the world's radioactive waste dump." The mill is also uphill from the Ute Mountain Ute Tribe. They fear the waste will get into their water supply. If it does, people will get sick. Radioactive waste causes cancer and other diseases.

One area of Utah's economy that has grown is tourism. In 2019 tourism was one of the top ten biggest industries in the state. Tourists spent more than $10 billion in the state that year. Utah's five national parks attract tourists from around the world. These include Bryce Canyon National Park and Zion National Park. The five parks recorded a total of more than 10 million visits in 2019.

Elsewhere in the state, tourists enjoy

More than 120,000 people attended the Sundance Film Festival in 2019.

skiing on the Rocky Mountains. Many resorts have opened in this area. Utah also hosts the Sundance Film Festival, an event where independent filmmakers screen their movies, which draws other people to the state.

FURTHER EVIDENCE

Chapter Four discusses some of Utah's industries. Mining is just one of many. What was one of the main points about mining in this chapter? What key evidence supports this point? Go to the article about mining at the website below. Find a quote from the website that supports the chapter's main point.

MINING

abdocorelibrary.com/utah

USA

CHAPTER FIVE

PEOPLE AND PLACES

Many famous people were born in Utah. They include winter sports stars such as Noelle Pikus-Pace. Pikus-Pace was born in Provo, Utah, and is an Olympian skeleton slider. She won a silver medal at the 2014 Winter Olympics in Sochi, Russia.

UTAH DEMOGRAPHICS

White people who are not Hispanic or Latino make up approximately 78 percent of Utah's population. But the state is home to

Noelle Pikus-Pace competes in skeleton racing at the 2014 Winter Olympics.

people of many races and ethnicities. Approximately 60,000 American Indians live in Utah. Some live on reservations, but not all do. The two Ute reservations in Utah are located in the northeast. Ten separate areas of land make up reservations for the Paiute Indian Tribe of Utah. The Navajo Reservation extends into Utah from Arizona. Individual tribes work to preserve their tribe's unique language and culture.

Latinos are the largest minority group in the state today. They make up 14 percent of Utah's population. They help shape the Utah government and give voice to their cultural beliefs.

East Asians first arrived in the mid-1800s for work. Today they celebrate their cultures at festivals. Their cultures are also expressed through traditional arts such as paper crafts and needlework.

IMPORTANT PLACES

Landscapes in Utah's national parks are hard or impossible to find anywhere else. One of the most famous examples is Arches National Park, which has more than 2,000 natural arches. These arches exist in part because the park gets little rain. What moisture the area does get helps shape these amazing formations.

Utah's lands also hold sites that are sacred to American Indian peoples. For example, Pueblo of Zuni people have traveled to the Bears Ears region for generations. Bears Ears is an important site for many nations with ties to the Ancestral Pueblo.

PERSPECTIVES

OVERCROWDING IN MOAB

Moab, Utah, is located near Arches National Park. Arches brings more than 3 million visitors to Moab a year. But fewer than 6,000 people are year-round residents of the city. Moab is not equipped to handle so many people. Tourists put stress on local resources. The county's emergency response department is overwhelmed with calls from tourists. Andy Nettell is a local business owner in Moab. He says, "I fear the locals are losing the quality of life many have moved here for, and that's quiet and solitude."

UTAH SYMPHONY

At the age of 44, Maurice Abravanel had already conducted for well-known opera houses. He wanted to build an orchestra of his own. In 1947, Abravanel began conducting with the brand-new Utah Symphony. For more than 30 years, he worked to grow the symphony. Today the Utah Symphony is respected as one of the top symphonies in the United States.

Mormon influence can be seen at the Salt Lake City Tabernacle. The tabernacle has some of the best acoustics in the country. A person in the back of the hall could hear a pin drop on the floor in the front. The famous Tabernacle Choir uses this space for its concerts.

For winter sports fans, Utah offers some of the best skiing in the United States. Salt Lake City hosted the Winter Olympics in 2002. The Olympic facilities in Park City are popular attractions. Tourists can ski or try bobsledding. Many winter sports athletes come to Park City to train.

The Bears Ears buttes and the area surrounding them are important sites for many American Indian nations in the region.

Utah has adventures for every person. Big cities offer museums and music. Mountains, rivers, and deserts provide scenic getaways. But Utah's cities and wilderness areas are not just beautiful places. They also help tell the exciting history of the state.

EXPLORE ONLINE

Chapter Five discusses a few of the places people can visit in Utah. One of these places is the Utah Olympic Park in Park City, Utah. As you know, every source is different. The website below has more information about all of the activities at the Utah Olympic Park. How is the information from the website the same as the information in Chapter Five? What new information did you learn from the website?

UTAH OLYMPIC PARK

abdocorelibrary.com/utah

IMPORTANT DATES

9000 BCE
First peoples settle in present-day Utah.

500 CE
Fremont culture develops in the northern region of Utah.

1150 CE
Ancestral Puebloans build cliff dwellings.

1820s
European traders begin to build fur trading posts in the region.

1847
The first groups of Latter-day Saints arrive in present-day Salt Lake City.

1865
The Ute people sign a treaty agreeing to move to a reservation.

1890
The Church of Jesus Christ of Latter-day Saints publishes a document banning the practice of polygamy.

1896
Utah becomes a state on January 4.

2002
Utah hosts the Winter Olympics in Salt Lake City.

STOP AND THINK

Surprise Me

Chapter Three discusses the plants and animals in Utah. After reading this book, what two or three facts about Utah's wildlife did you find most surprising? Write a few sentences about each fact. Why did you find each fact surprising?

Dig Deeper

After reading this book, what questions do you still have about Utah? With an adult's help, find a few reliable sources that can help you answer your questions. Write a paragraph about what you learned.

Take a Stand

Mining is an important part of Utah's economy. Some people believe uranium mines should open again. But other people believe the costs to Utah's environment are too high. Do you think mining companies should be allowed to open more mines in Utah? Or do you think it is important to keep some areas of the state protected? Why?

You Are There

This book discusses a few of the many different landscapes in Utah. Imagine you are traveling through the state. Write a letter home telling your friends what you have seen. What do you notice about the different kinds of landscapes? Be sure to add plenty of detail to your notes.

GLOSSARY

acoustics
how sounds bounce off surfaces in a building

ancestral
having to do with people from the past

culture
the way groups of people live; their customs, beliefs, and laws

elevation
the height above sea level

evaporate
to change from a liquid to a gas

radioactive
able to release dangerous energy

reservation
an area of land set aside for American Indian people

territory
an area of land that is not a state but is still controlled by a country

treaty
an official agreement between governments

ONLINE RESOURCES

To learn more about Utah, visit our free resource websites below.

Visit **abdocorelibrary.com** or scan this QR code for free Common Core resources for teachers and students, including vetted activities, multimedia, and booklinks, for deeper subject comprehension.

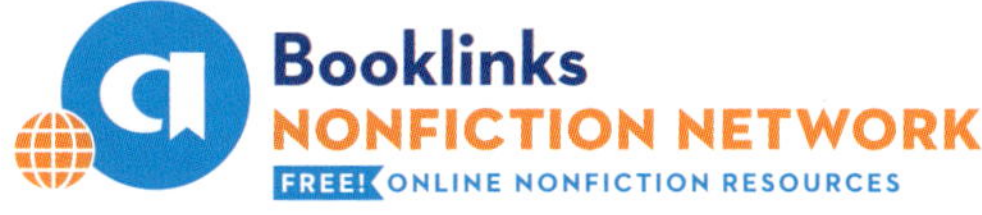

Visit **abdobooklinks.com** or scan this QR code for free additional online weblinks for further learning. These links are routinely monitored and updated to provide the most current information available.

LEARN MORE

Hamilton, John. *Utah: The Beehive State*. Abdo, 2017.

Mooney, Carla. *Traditional Stories of the Great Basin and Plateau Nations*. Abdo, 2018.

INDEX

About the Author

Martha London lives in Saint Paul, Minnesota. She writes children's books full time. When she isn't writing, you can find her hiking in the woods.